HAND SHADOWS
AND
MORE HAND SHADOWS
TO BE THROWN UPON THE WALL

FROM ORIGINAL DESIGNS BY
HENRY BURSILL

DOVER PUBLICATIONS, INC.
Mineola, New York

Published in Canada by General Publishing Company, Ltd., 30 Les-mill Road, Don Mills, Toronto, Ontario.

Published in the United Kingdom by Constable and Company, Ltd., 3 The Lanchesters, 162–164 Fulham Palace Road, London W6 9ER.

Bibliographical Note

This Dover edition, first published in 1997, is a slightly altered republication in one volume of the work originally published in two volumes by Dover Publications, Inc., in 1967 and 1971. The previous Dover editions were unabridged republications of the works first published by Griffith and Farran, London, in 1859 (Volume 1) and 1860 (Volume 2; under the title *Hand Shadows: Second Series*). The original prefaces to each edition written by Henry Bursill have been omitted for reasons of space. In addition, one repeated illustration, the original Griffith and Farran title page, and a list of contents in Volume 2 have all been omitted. The two original frontispieces have been placed on the inside front and back covers.

Library of Congress Cataloging-in-Publication Data

Bursill, Henry.
    [Hand shadows to be thrown upon the wall]
    Hand shadows and more hand shadows to be thrown upon the wall : a series of novel and amusing figures formed by the hand / from original designs by Henry Bursill.
       p.   cm.
    Originally published: Hand shadows to be thrown upon the wall. London : Griffith and Farran, 1859–1860.
    ISBN 0-486-29513-3 (pbk.)
    1. Shadow-pictures.   I. Title.
GV1218.S5B87   1997
791.5'3—dc21   96-48842
                                          CIP

Manufactured in the United States of America
Dover Publications, Inc., 31 East 2nd Street, Mineola, N.Y. 11501

THE GOOSE A PRISONER.

DEER.

Hy Burvill Invt Et Delt

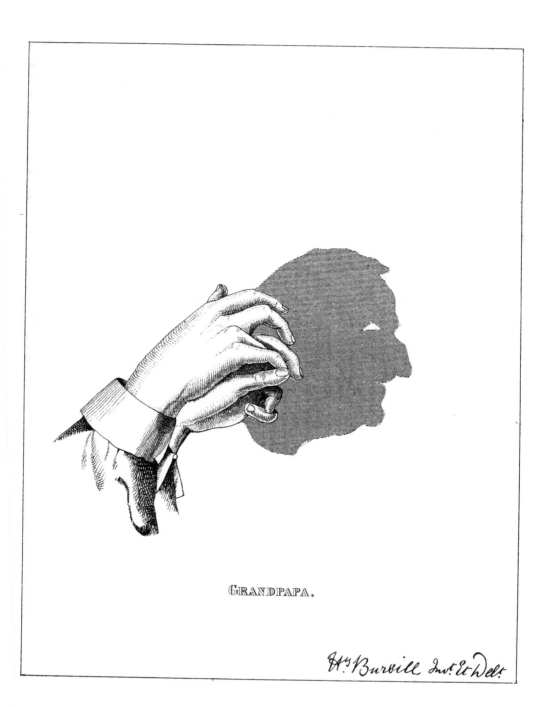

GRANDPAPA.

Hy Burvill Invt Et Delt

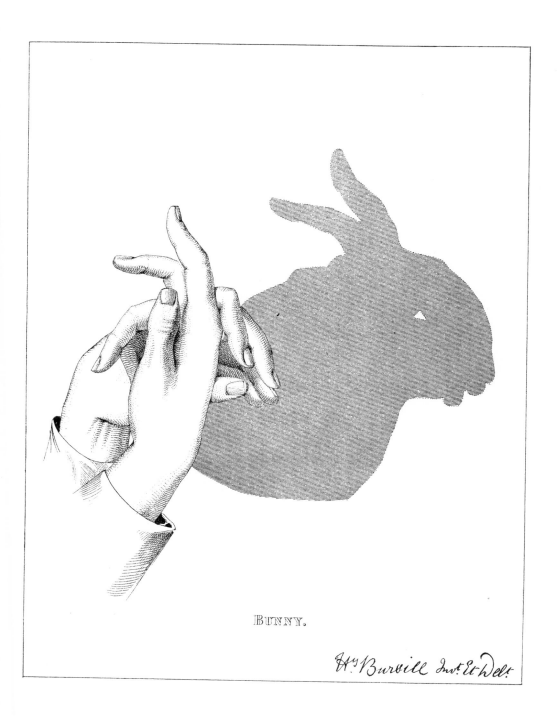

BUNNY.

Hy Burvill Invt Et Delt

A BIRD IN FLIGHT.

Hy Burvill Invt Et Delt

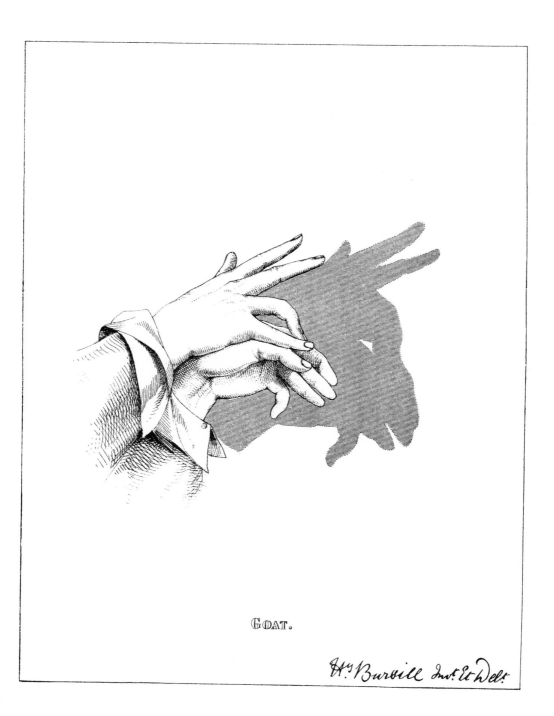

GOAT.

Hy Burvill Inv.t Et Del.t

DOG TOBY.

Hy Bursill Inv. Et Del.

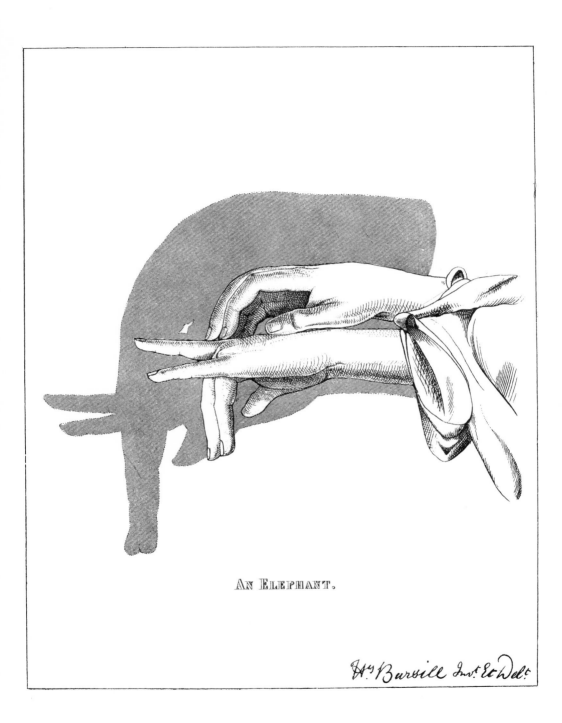

An Elephant.

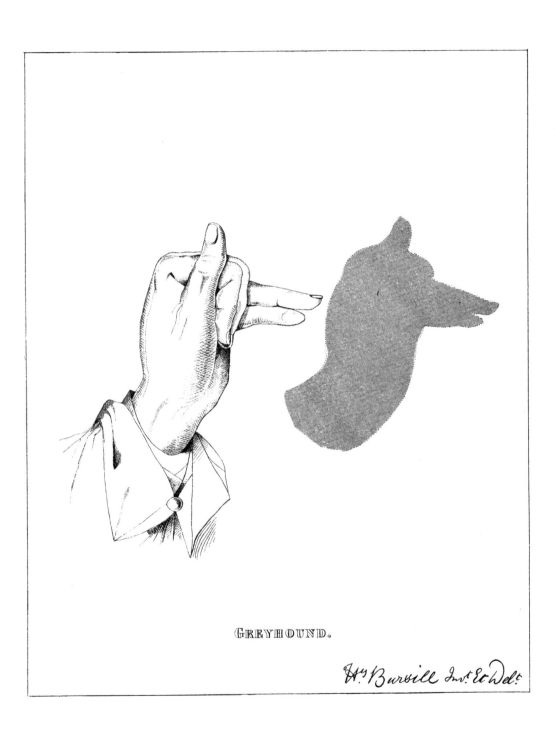

GREYHOUND.

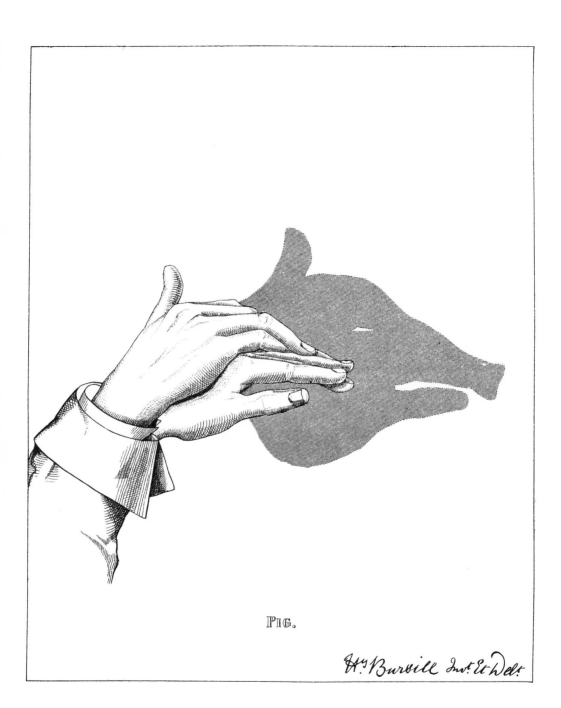

PIG.

Hy Burvill Inv.t Et Del.t

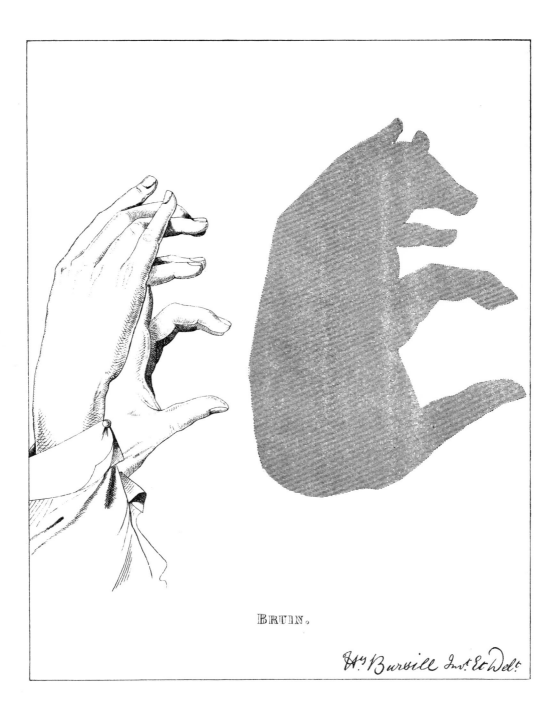

BRUIN.

Wm Bursill Invt Et Delt

A PORTRAIT.

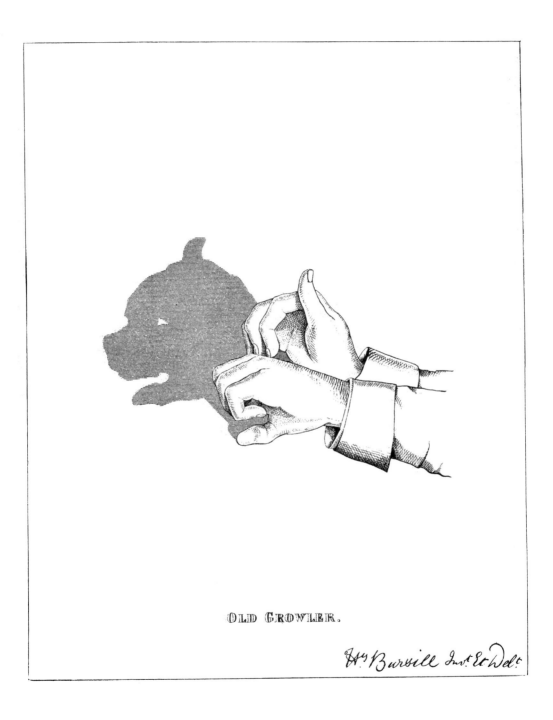

OLD GROWLER.

Hy Bursill Invt Et Delt

FRIGHT.

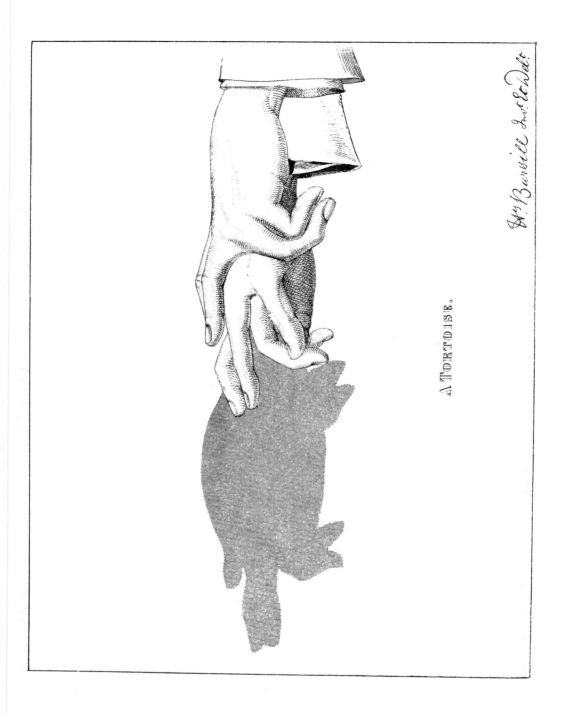

A TORTOISE.

Wm Burrell Inv.t & Del.t

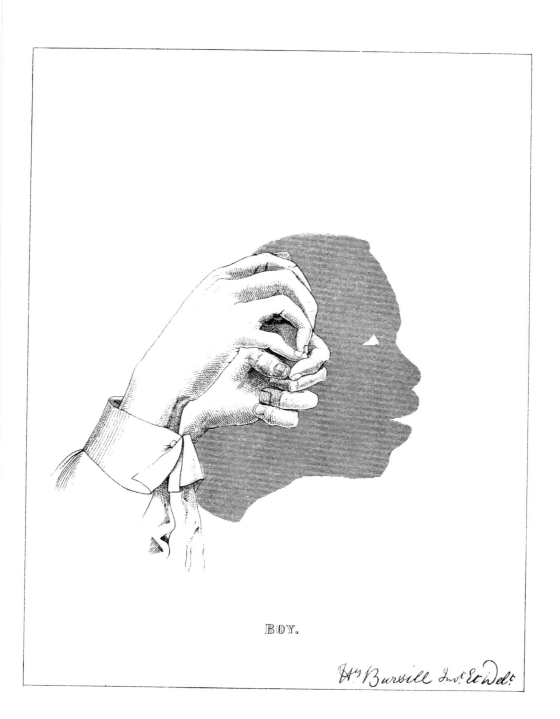

BOY.

H.^y Bursill Inv.^t Et Del.^t

WELLINGTON.

H. Bursill Delt

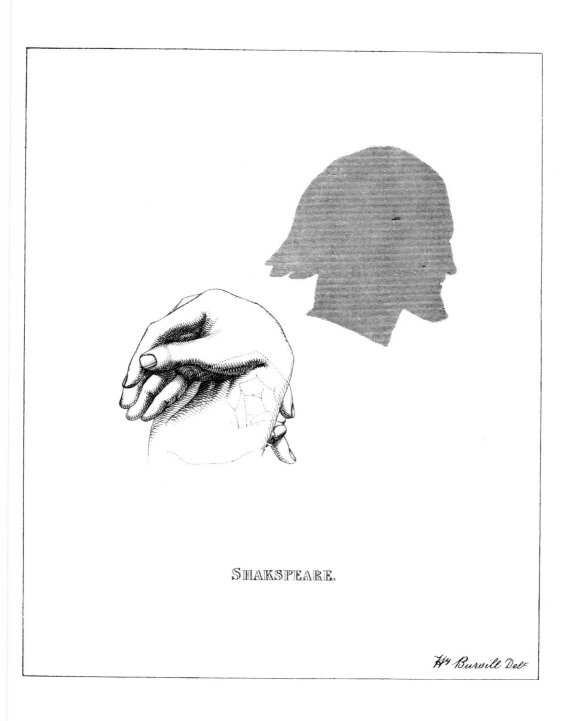

SHAKSPEARE.

HARE.

H. Bursill Del.

MIKE.

Wm Burvill Delt.

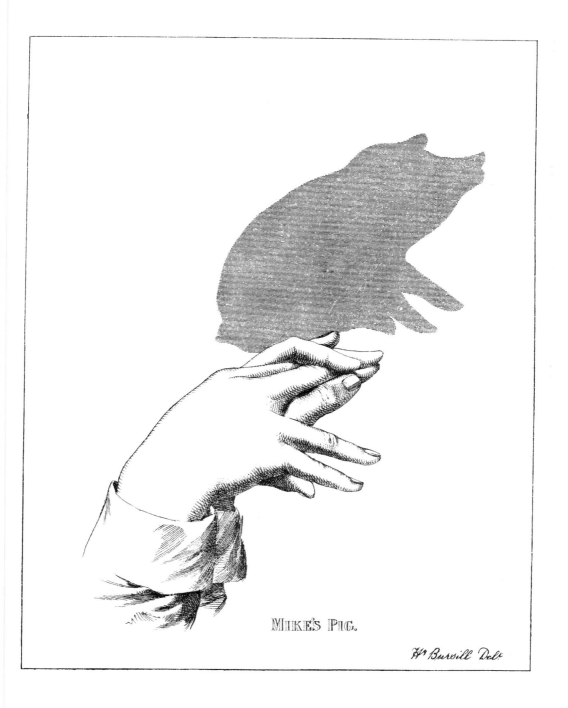

MIKE'S PIG.

Hy Burvill Delt

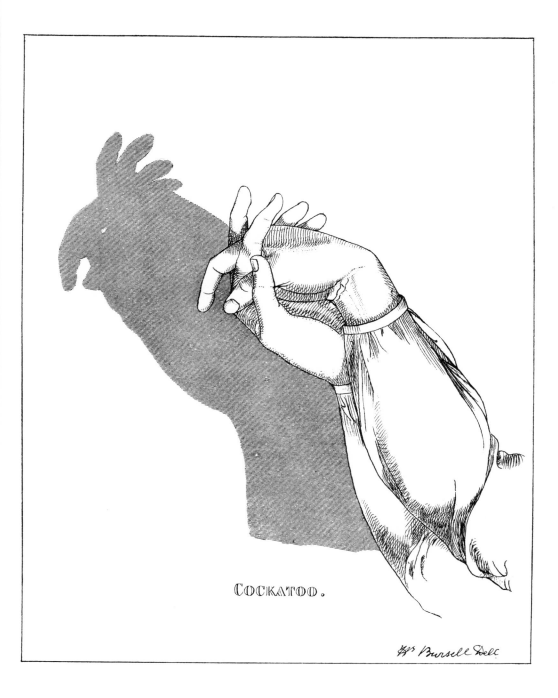

COCKATOO.

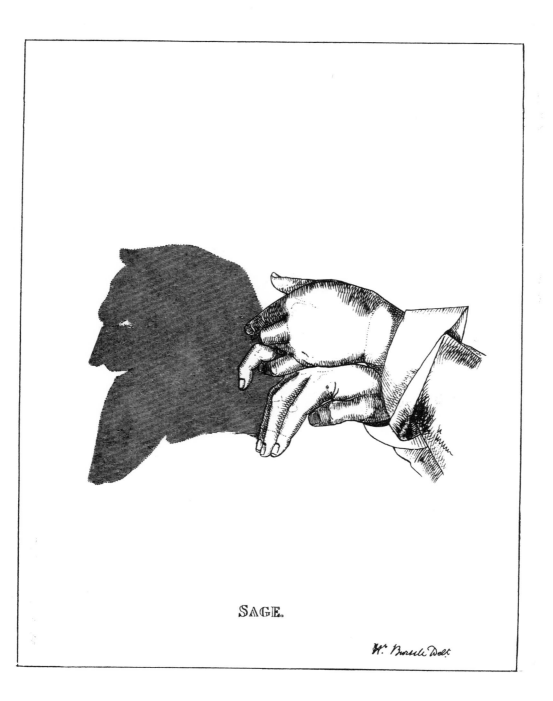

SAGE.

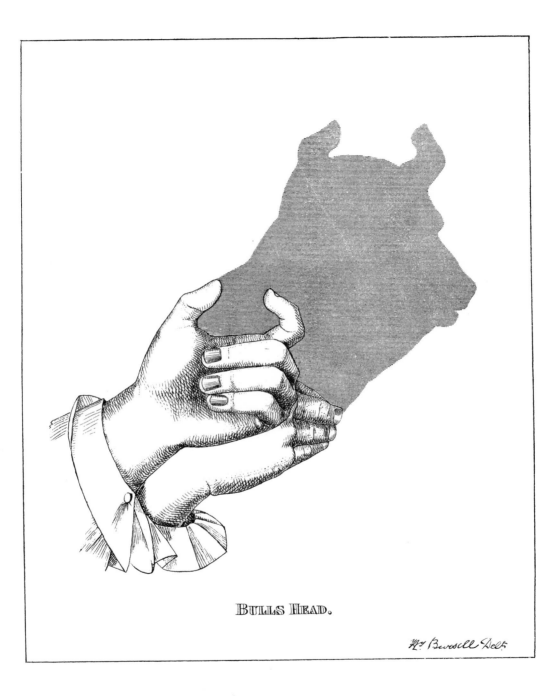

BULLS HEAD.

SQUIRREL.

H. Bursill Delt.

EAGLE.

W. Bartle Delt.

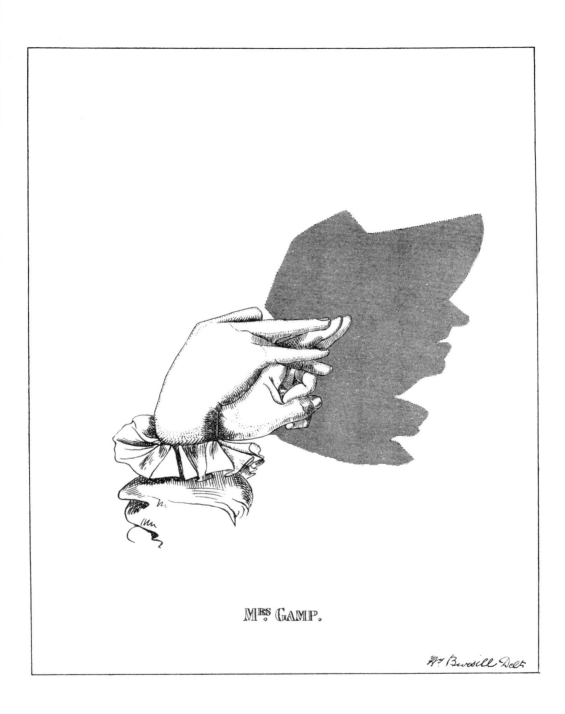

M^{RS}· GAMP.

SHEEP.

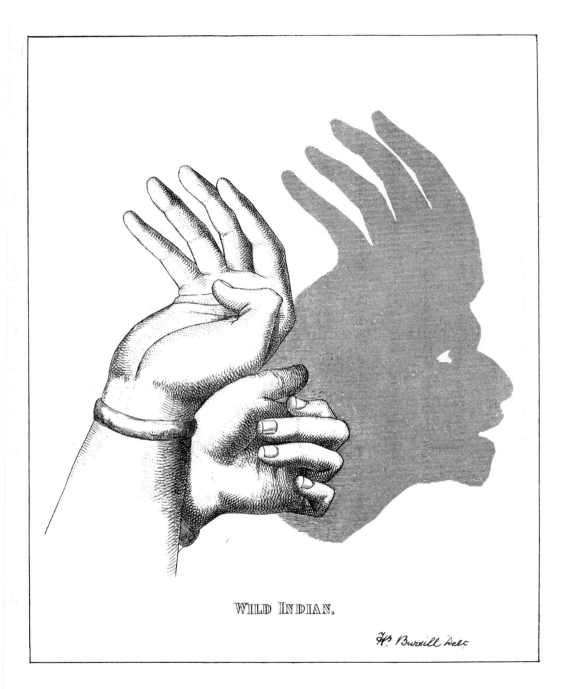

WILD INDIAN.

H⁵ Burrill delt.

MR. PUNCH.

A BLACK SWAN.

W. Burcill Delt.